**Please return/renew this item by the last date
shown
Thank you for using your library**

**REDCAR & CLEVELAND LIBRARY SERVICE**

# WORLD HABITATS

# RIVERS and LAKES

Rose Pipes

A ZOË BOOK

## A ZOË BOOK

© 1997 Zoë Books Limited

Devised and produced by
Zoë Books Limited
15 Worthy Lane
Winchester
Hampshire SO23 7AB
England

First published in Great Britain in 1997 by
Zoë Books Limited
15 Worthy Lane
Winchester
Hampshire SO23 7AB

A record of the CIP data is available from the British Library.

ISBN 1 86173 013 6

Printed in Italy by Grafedit SpA
Editor: Kath Davies
Artwork: Cecilia Fitzsimons
Map: Sterling Associates
Design & Production: Sterling Associates

## Photographic acknowledgments

The publishers wish to acknowledge, with thanks, the following photographic sources:

Robert Harding Picture Library / Robert Estall 15; / Bildagentur Schuster 19; The Hutchison Library / Eric Lawrie - cover inset bl; Impact Photos / Homer Sykes - title page; / Mark Henley 9; / Colin Jones 11, 12; / Yann Arthus Bertrand 13; / Neil Morrison 14; / Robert Gibbs 23; Philip A.Sauvain 20; South American Pictures / Peter Dixon 22; / Tony Morrison 24; Still Pictures / Andre Bartschi - cover background; / Hartmut Schwarzbach 4, 8, 26; / J.P.Sylvestre 17; / Gil Moti 27; / Roland Seitre 28; / Hjalte Tin 29; TRIP / P. Joynson-Hicks 10; / © Viesti Associates 16; / TH-Foto Werbung 18; Zefa - cover inset tr, 7, 21, 25.

The publishers have made every effort to trace the copyright holders, but if they have inadvertently overlooked any, they will be pleased to make the necessary arrangement at the first opportunity.

# Contents

# What and where are rivers and lakes?

The river in this picture starts, or rises, in the Himalayan Mountains of Nepal. It ends its long journey in the Bay of Bengal.

Rivers carry fresh water from high ground down to the sea. Many rivers start as small streams, and some begin as melting ice. Lakes are large pools of water.

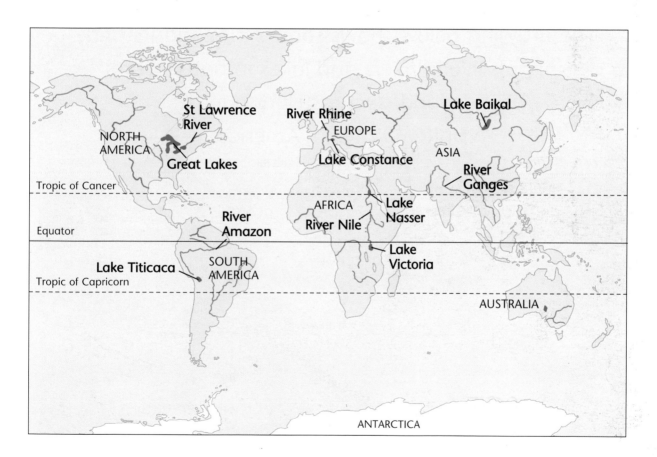

Some of the largest lakes and the longest rivers in the world are on this map. It shows all the rivers and lakes that you will read about in this book.

# Wildlife in rivers and lakes

The plants and animals that live in rivers and lakes are well **adapted** to living in or beside fresh water **habitats**.

The drawing below shows some of the plants and animals live in rivers and lakes in hotter parts of the world, such as Florida in the United States of America.

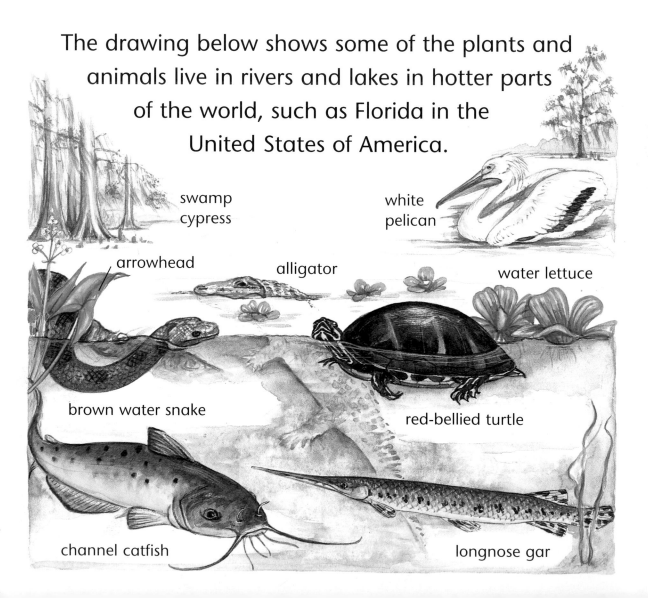

swamp cypress

white pelican

arrowhead

alligator

water lettuce

brown water snake

red-bellied turtle

channel catfish

longnose gar

This salmon is jumping up a waterfall. The brown bear eats salmon. The bear waits until a fish jumps out of the water, then catches the fish in its mouth.

The drawing below shows some plants and animals that live in rivers and lakes in cooler parts of the world.

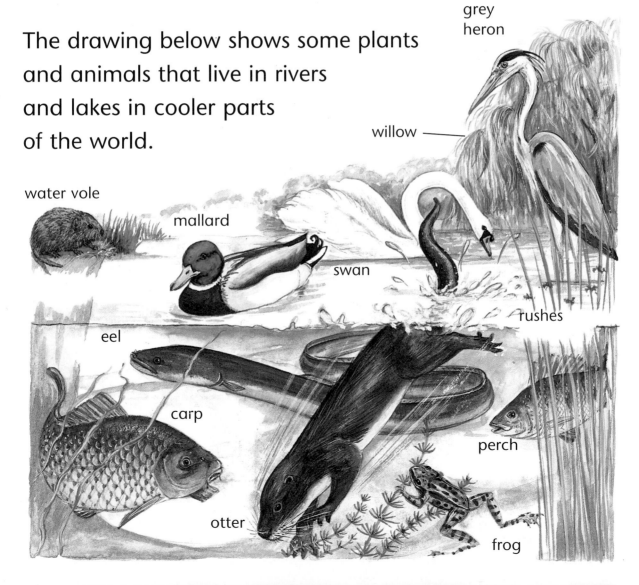

grey heron

willow

water vole

mallard

swan

rushes

eel

carp

perch

otter

frog

# Using rivers and lakes

Many rivers and lakes are important highways. Ships carry people and goods from one place to another.

The Chinese city of Shanghai is on the River Huangpu. Shanghai is a river **port**. Ships use the river to travel to other parts of China.

We use water from rivers and lakes to drink and to water, or **irrigate**, the land. Water is also used to produce electricity.

People visit rivers and lakes for holidays. On rocky rivers, people enjoy canoeing and white-water rafting.

Lake Geneva, in Switzerland, is popular for water sports such as boating, swimming and water skiing.

# The River Nile and Lake Victoria in Africa

The River Nile runs for 6670 kilometres through Africa. The River Nile begins its long journey in Lake Victoria.

Lake Victoria is the largest lake in Africa. There are many villages like this one beside the lake.

The River Nile flows through hills, lakes, swamps and deserts. It flows north to the Mediterranean Sea.

Africa's largest **freshwater** fish is the Nile perch. Perch can grow to about two metres.

These men are fishing in the Nile in Sudan. There are many different kinds of fish to catch.

Another large river animal is the Nile crocodile. A crocodile as long as five metres was once seen in Lake Victoria!

People lived on the Nile's banks in Egypt more than 5000 years ago. Their temples and tombs can still be seen.

The Nile's waters are used for drinking, and for irrigating **crops**. Without the Nile, the land would be a desert.

The River Nile splits into many smaller **channels** near the sea. There are islands of land between the channels. The area is called a **delta**. Farmers grow vegetables in the rich soil of the delta.

This picture was taken from an aircraft. You can see the delta farmland and the city of Alexandria on the coast.

# The Saint Lawrence River and the Great Lakes in North America

The five Great Lakes in North America were formed about 250,000 years ago by moving ice, or **glaciers**.

The River Niagara flows between Lake Erie and Lake Ontario. The huge waterfalls on this river are called the Niagara Falls. One side of the falls is in Canada, the other is in the United States of America.

There are **rapids** in the Saint Lawrence River. Ships cannot sail through rapids, so people built **canals** to go around them.

The Saint Lawrence Seaway runs between Lake Erie and Montreal in Canada. Ships can sail along the Seaway from the Great Lakes all the way to the Atlantic Ocean.

This is the Welland Canal. It is part of the Saint Lawrence Seaway.

Ships carry oil and grain from the Great Lakes ports along the Saint Lawrence Seaway. These loads, or cargoes, are sold across the world.

Duluth is a port on Lake Superior in the USA. You can see a tanker on the lake.

Near the sea, the Saint Lawrence River contains fresh water and salty sea water. Many different kinds of whale live here.

Hunting whales is not allowed now, but the whales are still in danger. This is because the river water is dirty, or **polluted**.

This is a beluga whale. People hunted these whales for their oil.

# The River Rhine and Lake Constance in Europe

The Rhine is the longest river in Europe. It rises in the Swiss Alps, and flows for 1320 km through seven countries to the North Sea.

Many tourists visit Lake Constance. They can sail, swim or fish in the lake, and the scenery is beautiful.

Near the busy Swiss river port of Basel, the Rhine turns north. It flows between the Vosges mountains in France, and the Black Forest mountains in Germany.

Between Bingen and Bonn, the river flows through a narrow valley, or **gorge**.

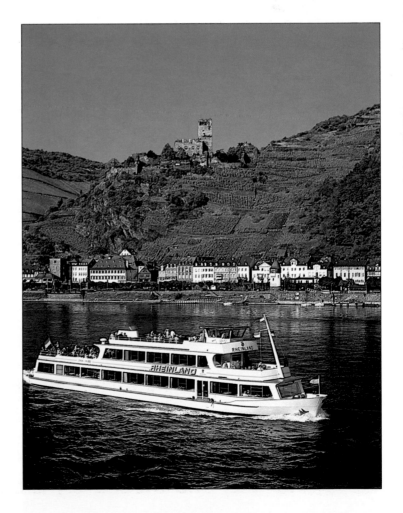

There are castles on the hillsides, and vineyards where grapes grow. Tourists take trips on the river in this part of the Rhine gorge.

The Rhine enters the North Sea near Rotterdam in the Netherlands. Barges unload their cargoes at this port. From there, ships take the cargoes around the world.

This long, flat boat is a Rhine barge. The barges carry heavy cargoes such as coal and stone. The busiest part of the Rhine is near Cologne and Duisburg, where there are many factories.

21

The Rhine used to be a very badly polluted river.

In 1986, chemicals spilled into the river from a Swiss factory. They poisoned half a million fish, as well as eels, insects and waterbirds. Even sheep and cows were poisoned because they drank the river water.

The river is cleaner now, and the wildlife is coming back.

These fish died because the river water was polluted.

# The River Amazon and Lake Titicaca in South America

More than 3000 kinds of fish live in the River Amazon, and some large **mammals** such as the Amazon river dolphin. Some of the forest peoples live close to the river, where they catch fish to eat.

The River Amazon flows for 6488 km through thick rainforest across South America.

The city of Manaus is in the middle of the rainforest, where the River Amazon joins the River Negro. The river is deep and wide here.

Ships can sail from Manaus for 1600 km to the Atlantic Ocean. They carry rainforest **products** such as timber, rubber and Brazil nuts.

Ships load goods at the river port of Manaus.

Lake Titicaca is in the Andes Mountains.
It is the biggest lake in South America.

Lake Titicaca is the highest large lake in the world.
Part of the lake is in Bolivia. The other part is in Peru.

People have lived beside Lake Titicaca for thousands of years. There are plenty of fish and wild animals to catch and eat. The water reeds are useful for making boats, houses and many other things.

Huge flocks of waterbirds live on or visit the lake. Many birds live among the reeds that grow at the edge of the water.

You can see reed boats and houses in this picture.

# The River Ganges in Asia

Most Indian people belong to the **Hindu** religion. To Hindus, the Ganges is a holy river. People visit cities such as Varanasi to bathe in the river's waters.

The River Ganges runs through northern India to the sea in Bangladesh. People who live on the river's banks catch fish, wash clothes, and bathe in the water.

Farmers use the Ganges river water to irrigate crops in the dry season. In the rainy season, the river floods the land. The flood water leaves rich soil behind it.

Floods can also be very dangerous. Thousands of people may die or lose their homes when the river floods.

This picture shows a flooded village street in Bangladesh.

# Lake Baikal in Siberia

Lake Baikal is more than 1.5km deep. It is the oldest, deepest lake in the world.

This beautiful lake is home to many different kinds of animal. Baikal seals are found nowhere else in the world.

Lake Baikal is a long way inland. Winters there are very cold, and from January to May, the lake freezes over.

Forests grow all around Lake Baikal. Wood from the trees is made into pulp and paper in mills on the lakeside.

The mills used to dump their waste into Lake Baikal. It poisoned the fish and other lake creatures. Now the waste is cleaned before it enters the lake.

A papermill on Lake Baikal

# Glossary

**adapted:** if a plant or an animal can find everything it needs to live in a place, we say that it has adapted to that place. The animals can find food and shelter, and the plants have enough food in the soil and enough water. Some animals have changed their shape or their colour over a long time, so that they can catch food or hide easily. Some plants in dry areas can store water in their stems or roots.

**canals:** straight waterways, built to carry boats and barges.

**channels:** waterways. A river sometimes splits into smaller streams or channels as it reaches the sea.

**crops:** plants which farmers grow to use or to sell.

**delta:** a triangle-shaped piece of land at the mouth of a river. The river often breaks up into channels when it crosses a delta.

**freshwater:** water that is not salty.

**glacier:** a thick, tongue-shaped mass of ice. Glaciers form in valleys, and move very slowly downhill.

**gorge:** a deep, narrow opening in the ground. It often has a stream or river at the bottom.

**habitat:** the natural home of a plant or animal. Examples of habitats are deserts, forests and grasslands.

**Hindu:** someone who follows the Hindu religion. Hindus believe that their religion shows them a way to get closer to God. There are many gods, goddesses and festivals in this religion.

**irrigate:** to water crops.

**mammals**: the group of animals whose young feed on their mother's milk.

**polluted**: poisoned. Polluted water may be dangerous to wildlife.

**port:** a town where ships load and unload goods. Ports are next to rivers, lakes or the sea.

**products:** crops that we grow or goods that we make.

**rapids:** where a river runs very fast over rocks or down a slope.

# Index